ETHICS IN BUSINESS: A GUIDE FOR MANAGERS

Dorothy J. Maddux
Robert B. Maddux

A FIFTY-MINUTE™ SERIES BOOK

CRISP PUBLICATIONS, INC.
Menlo Park, California

ETHICS IN BUSINESS: A GUIDE FOR MANAGERS

Dorothy J. Maddux

Robert B. Maddux

CREDITS
Editor: **Marian Sanders**
Designer: **Carol Harris**
Typesetting: **Interface Studio**
Cover Design: **Carol Harris**
Artwork: **Ralph Mapson**

Copyright © 1989 by Crisp Publications, Inc.
Printed in the United States of America

Distribution to the U.S. Trade:

National Book Network, Inc.
4720 Boston Way
Lanham, MD 20706
1-800-462-6420

Library of Congress Catalog Card Number 88-63799
Maddux, Dorothy J; Maddux, Robert B.
Ethics in Business
ISBN 0-931961-69-6

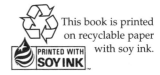

This book is printed on recyclable paper with soy ink.

PREFACE

The primary role of a manager includes setting and administering policy, solving problems and making decisions. In so doing, countless factors are analyzed, evaluated, and interpreted. Employees, customers and competitors, as well as the productivity of the business, are affected by the results.

Do these results enhance the business and the lives of those they affect? Do they reflect the ethical principles expected by the organization and demanded by society? Do companies have ethical standards governing the way they conduct their business and interact with employees, customers, competitors, suppliers, and the general public? If so, are these standards communicated to, and understood by, managers and employees? Does anyone care?

There is abundant evidence that people and organizations do care. A recent Bentley College survey of the Fortune 500 industrial and 500 service companies found that almost 75 percent had codes of ethics. In addition, 35 percent were providing employee training in ethics, 14 percent had ethics committees and 6 percent had ethics omsbudsmen. Public opinion polls, however, reflect real concerns about the integrity of those in business. A Gallup poll taken the same time as the Bentley survey mentioned above, found that half of those interviewed believed business values were declining. In a Harris survey conducted that same year, only 18 percent expressed ''great confidence'' in the leaders of major companies. This was down from 27 percent in the early 1970's and 55 percent in 1966.

Wrong is frequently committed by well-meaning people simply because they have never given serious thought to an issue one way or the other. They conform without question to what appears to be ''the way things are done.'' There are many managers who, as far as ethics are concerned, operate in a void. They have not thought issues through in light of their ethical implications.

Situations often arise that are so complex it seems impossible for even the most ethically aware people to find their way. Decisions frequently have to be made quickly with limited data; one set of demands may press hard in one direction, another in the other. Good and bad, or right and wrong, are not always easily discerned.

PREFACE (Continued)

Managers working in essentially authoritarian organizations often find little latitude in which to question, or challenge, the thrust of a policy or strategy. Resistance in any form may put them at risk. These factors contribute to the creation and poor management of ethical dilemmas.

The personal characteristics of managers, developed over the years as a result of their life experience, greatly influence the degree to which they recognize ethical dilemmas, and the extent to which they become concerned with their proper resolution.

The list of factors that make ethical management difficult goes on and on. Enough have been enumerated, however, to demonstrate that managerial concerns about ethics are not just limited to laws, regulations, and rules that have been carefully studied, interpreted and written down for easy reference. Managers must contend with ethical dilemmas arising from far more subtle issues like performance appraisals, product quality, safety, discrimination, customer relations, salary administration, communication, and discipline. These are areas that have many nuances and implications, but frequently no clear-cut answers.

This book is intended to help managers recognize and think through ethical issues when they arise, and to contribute to their overall knowledge of the management process. The honesty, integrity and good will of those who manage an organization set the stage for effective and profitable results.

Dorothy J. Maddux   Robert B. Maddux

CONTENTS

PART I
UNDERSTANDING THE
PROBLEM AND THE NEED

GETTING ETHICAL CONSIDERATIONS IN BALANCE

SOME IMPORTANT OBJECTIVES FOR THE READER

Before you begin this book, give some thought to your objectives.

Objectives give us a sense of direction, a definition of what we plan to accomplish and a feeling of fulfillment when they are achieved.

Check the objectives below that are important to you. Then, when you have completed this book, review your objectives and enjoy the sense of achievement you will feel.

AFTER LEARNING AND PRACTICING CONCEPTS PRESENTED IN THIS BOOK, YOU WILL BE ABLE TO:

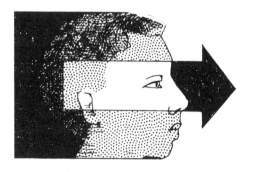

☑ recognize the ethical implications of issues as they arise.

☑ examine ethical dilemmas objectively and apply reasoned judgement to their resolution.

☑ correct unethical practices that may have previously been unrecognized or ignored.

☑ handle ethical dilemmas that could affect personal relationships diplomatically.

☑ communicate the need for applying ethical principles at all organizational levels.

WHAT DO WE MEAN BY ETHICS?

You are about to undertake a brief study of ethics in management. You already have an interest in this subject or you wouldn't be reading this book. Perhaps you have questions about just what the term "ETHICS" means in a managerial setting or how "ETHICAL PRINCIPLES" can be followed in an organization over which you have limited control.

You probably want to learn more about how to handle yourself well when faced with ethical dilemmas so that your organization is properly represented, your relationships are preserved and your conscience is clear.

Let's start by comparing some of your ideas with those of the authors.

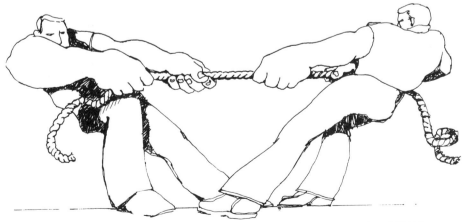

SOME ETHICAL ISSUES ARE LIKE A TUG OF WAR

YOUR IDEAS ABOUT ETHICS

1. In the space below, write what the word "ethics" means to you.

   _____

   _____

   _____

   _____

2. What are some of the specific ethical situations you encounter and must work through from time to time on the job?

   _____

   _____

   _____

   _____

   _____

   _____

3. How frequently are you involved in situations where ethics are an appropriate concern?

   ☐ Very rarely

   ☐ Almost every day

   ☐ A few times each year

   ☐ Never

NOW LOOK ON THE NEXT PAGE AND COMPARE YOUR THOUGHTS WITH THOSE OF THE AUTHORS.

DEFINITIONS OF ETHICS

Webster's New World Dictionary, 3rd College Edition defines ''ethics'' as relating to what is good or bad, and having to do with moral duty and obligation. (''Moral'' is defined as relating to principles of right and wrong.)

''In a general sense,'' Dr. Albert Schweitzer said, ''ethics is the name we give to our concern for good behavior. We feel an obligation to consider not only our own personal well-being, but also that of others and of human society as a whole.'' Ethics is a way of being human. If early men and women had not identified their own welfare with that of others, they could not have survived and developed.

Business ethics involves being fully aware of what we're doing, including the consequences and complications of our actions. Being ethical in business requires acting with an awareness of:

- ☑ The need for complying with rules, such as the laws of the land, the customs and expectations of the community, the principles of morality, the policies of the organization and such general concerns as the needs of others and fairness.

- ☑ How the products and services of an organization, and the actions of its members, can affect its employees, the community and society as a whole, either positively or negatively.

*DO ETHICAL QUESTIONS EVER
CAUSE YOU TO DO THIS?*

ETHICAL CONCERNS OF MANAGERS

Public concerns about ethical practices in business usually relate to issues like embezzlement, accepting bribes or poisoning the atmosphere. Such examples suggest managers' problems with ethics consist of nothing more than violations of clear-cut, well-defined laws, rules, and codes of conduct.

Managers, on the other hand, mostly cite examples that arise directly from routine business practices. Their ethical concerns are about relationships and responsibilities where correct decisions are not perfectly clear, and there are no hard, fast rules to follow.

One set of relationships and responsibilities is directly related to employees, and includes such areas as discipline, performance appraisal, safety, and the administration of reward systems. Another set is concerned with customers and suppliers, and includes the intricate aspects of such elements as timing, quality, and price. Ethical dilemmas also arise when managers have conflicts in values with superiors or peers over such things as strategy, goals, policy, and administration.

Whatever the viewpoint, good ethics mean good business. Successful organizations and managers take ethics seriously. They reason their way through ethical dilemmas to acceptable solutions. Some organizations and managers give the appearance of success for long periods in spite of hidden unethical practices. The news is replete, however, with stories of the fallen heroes and devastated organizations that ultimately result from this deception.

ANY TIME YOU'RE DEALING WITH ISSUES OF RIGHTS AND FAIRNESS, YOU'RE DEALING WITH AN ETHICAL PROBLEM!

IDENTIFYING YOUR ETHICAL CONCERNS

Many managers report that the ethical dilemmas they face are difficult because they involve relationships with people (employees, peers, and bosses) with whom they have to work and on whom they are dependent. The dilemma is further complicated by the fact that these critical people may have contrary goals and competing needs. A mistep in handling an ethical issue may well affect a relationship, or linger on the conscience, for years to come.

When managers resolve ethical issues they must contend with the reaction of others within the organization who may be affected by the outcome. Will their judgment and response enhance or detract from the image the manager wishes to project?

The next page lists the ethical concerns of some managers. Read them carefully. Do you see them as ethical issues? If yes, do you deal with them effectively? If no, do you need to sharpen your awareness?

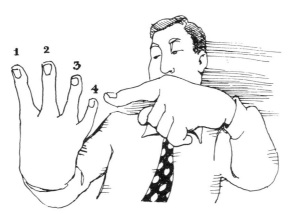

HOW MANY ETHICAL CONCERNS
CAN YOU IDENTIFY?

WHAT'S BOTHERING YOU?

In the following list of items, check those that bother you from an ethical standpoint. Circle the number on the rating scale that reflects the level of your concern. Five is the highest degree and one the lowest. If you have additional concerns, add them in the space provided.

	HIGH			LOW	
☐ Making decisions affecting employees' lives	5	4	3	2	1
☐ Administering some company policies	5	4	3	2	1
☐ Supporting some "unwritten" company policies	5	4	3	2	1
☐ Resolving employee grievances	5	4	3	2	1
☐ Administering budgets	5	4	3	2	1
☐ Assigning people to hazardous work	5	4	3	2	1
☐ Disrupting the work of others because of animosity or conflict between groups	5	4	3	2	1
☐ Misrepresenting issues to others	5	4	3	2	1
☐ Withholding important data to "protect" others	5	4	3	2	1
☐ Covering up drug/alcohol abuse among employees, peers and senior managers	5	4	3	2	1
☐ Controlling sexual harassment and other forms of employee discrimination	5	4	3	2	1
☐ Assigning work for reasons other than employees' qualifications	5	4	3	2	1
☐ Making it "rough" for employees so they will quit	5	4	3	2	1
☐ Submitting incorrect reports or altering records	5	4	3	2	1
☐ Permitting substandard quality in products or service	5	4	3	2	1
☐ Deferring action on health and safety issues	5	4	3	2	1
☐ "Stealing" or permitting others to "steal" or misuse company time, tools or materials	5	4	3	2	1
_____	5	4	3	2	1
_____	5	4	3	2	1

Any item you checked or added, especially those you rated 3 or higher, deserves careful attention. You may have some serious problems brewing. Start solving your ethical concerns now. This book is a good place to begin.

THE IMPLICATIONS OF MANAGERIAL ACTIONS

Managers sometimes appear to lose their perspective when making decisions that affect people. Perhaps they are very busy, or maybe they just don't take time to think through the implications of their actions. It seems unlikely they have not had some ethical training. Whatever the reason, the outcome is the same—an employee or group of employees, ends up being treated arbitrarily and unfairly. Ethics are sacrificed for the expedient accomplishment of a goal.

Once a senior manager makes a decision, it is remarkable how often other managers act as if there is no need to examine its ethical overtones. Ethics have somehow been suspended from evaluation for this particular event. The same is true when several managers with a stake in the outcome agree on an unfounded course of action. It's almost as if the group's agreement on a decision eliminates the need to examine it in terms of right and wrong.

When such decisions are "sanitized" of all ethical considerations, everyone loses. Managers fail themselves and all employees by doing less than their best, and the organization suffers a heavy blow to its credibility as an ethical member of the business community.

ARE YOU AND YOUR ASSOCIATES THINKING THROUGH THE ETHICAL IMPLICATIONS OF YOUR ACTIONS OR ARE YOU FREE-FALLING THROUGH AN ETHICAL VOID?

AS A MANAGER, IT IS ESSENTIAL THAT YOU DO NOT LOSE YOUR ETHICAL PERSPECTIVE WHEN MAKING DECISIONS

CASE STUDY I

Harass Him Until He Quits

Case studies help provide understanding and knowledge you may not already possess. Therefore, several case problems are included in this book. Please give each one your careful attention. The first case is not unusual, and the manager's solution is often seen as acceptable. What are the ethical implications of this manager's approach to working with people? What would you have done?

Rex Crane is 63 years old and has been with his organization for 26 years. He has had a varied career, and possesses a number of skills and abilities. Rex is quite set in his ways and somewhat eccentric. His supervisor and other senior managers would like to see him retire or let him go, but his performance meets the standards of the organization in all respects and he has no interest in retirement. No one has been able to identify any deficiencies that would warrant discharge.

The senior manager in Rex's department recently decided to create a work environment for Rex that would be so uncomfortable that it would ultimately cause Rex to quit. He presented the idea to Rex's immediate supervisor who accepted the idea readily. They began to give Rex thankless assignments and assigning him to the "graveyard" shift. Younger employees with less experience and service were given better assignments and shifts. Rex appealed the decision, but was told by his manager that "the assignments have all been made; if you don't like yours you can look elsewhere." There is no union or employee problem-solving process.

What are the ethical factors here?

_____

_____

Indicate how you would have handled this situation if you had been the immediate supervisor.

_____

_____

Please turn to page 65 for the authors' comments.

PART II
FORCES THAT SHAPE ETHICAL BEHAVIOR

WHEN AND WHERE DO WE DEVELOP ETHICAL VALUES?

How would you answer the following questions?

YES	NO	
☐	☐	Are we born knowing right from wrong?
☐	☐	Do our values develop in a vacuum?
☐	☐	Is there a time in our lives when our ethical values are ''set''— when we know, from that time on, the ethical basis on which to make decisions in our lives?

According to those who study the history and philosophy of ethics, infants would not survive without a nurturer (and begin to learn what that nurturer) who teaches them about right and wrong behavior. In human society, a series of nurturers and teachers influence the ethical views of each individual.

HUMAN HISTORY IS DEFINED BY THE CHOICES INDIVIDUALS MAKE. From the beginning human beings have been puzzled with ethical questions: ''What should we do? What should we not do?'' They have struggled to develop a system that produces the greatest good for the individual and for the group.

Over time, codes of conduct were developed to insure survival. These codes included the nurturing of children, forming of family and tribal units, and hunting rituals. Even the earliest people realized that there was danger of extinction if violent acts were not curtailed, if thievery went unhampered, if no one could count on anyone else to exercise the ''right'' behavior. Thus, a system of acceptable behavior was formed.

SOURCES OF ETHICAL VALUES

Since nurturers and role models give us the criteria we use to make ethical decisions, it is worthwhile to consider which individuals or institutions have influenced you. Please complete the exercise below. Norms of ethical behavior have developed throughout the ages in all cultures. Listed below are several of the philosophies, institutions, and individuals that have influenced human society. Check each that you believe has to one degree or another influenced your conduct.

- ☐ Mother

- ☐ Father

- ☐ Sibling

- ☐ Other Relative

- ☐ Friend

- ☐ Mentor

- ☐ Religious Leader

- ☐ Religious Writings

- ☐ Educators

- ☐ Youth Groups

- ☐ Sports Hero

- ☐ Military Hero

- ☐ Professional Hero

- ☐ Books—Essays—Philosophical Writings

- ☐ Other

_____

_____

ETHICS AND YOUR JOB

An individual's ethical viewpoint does not develop or exist apart from the ''real'' world. Values developed in childhood and youth are constantly tested and on-the-job decisions reflect the employee's understanding of ethical responsibility.

An individual's ethical behavior affects not only his or her reputation within the company, but may also contribute to the way in which the company is perceived by others.

On the facing page, check those ethical standards that you believe apply to your job.

ETHICAL VALUES ON THE JOB

Business ethics cannot be separated from ethics in general and the individual must deal with job problems on the basis of fundamental ethical standards. The list below names several commonly accepted ethical values of our society. What importance do you think each has in your job?

	Very Important	Somewhat Important	Not Important
Honesty			
Fairness			
Obedience to the law			
Compassion			
Respect for others			
Loyalty			
Dependability			
Courage			
Helpfulness			
Self-control			
Truthfulness			

> . . .THE GOLDEN RULE WAS MEANT FOR BUSINESS AS MUCH AS FOR OTHER HUMAN RELATIONSHIPS.
>
> J. Cash Penney, Founder,
> *J.C. Penney Company*

FACTORS THAT MODIFY ETHICAL VALUES

Honesty, truthfulness, loyalty, respect—most of us have seen the relevance of these qualities to the way we do our job. However, we can also think of situations in gray areas that make decisions difficult on an ethical basis.

For instance, we believe that honesty is essential in business, and would never steal money from the cash drawer, but...

We use the company car to run personal errands while making sales rounds.

We observe working hours scrupulously and often put in overtime, so

telling the boss we got caught in traffic, when we actually overslept, seems innocent enough.

We give our best to the company and work hard, so...

gossiping about my supervisor to fellow employees just helps me let off a little steam.

We know our co-worker is running a small business of her own on the side, using the office telephone, copier, typewriter, paper—and time.

But we've been friends for years, and she's a single parent with a son in college. It's unlikely she'll be caught if we don't inform anyone.

> ON THE FACING PAGE CHECK THOSE JOB SITUATIONS WHICH WOULD TEST YOUR ETHICAL STANDARDS.

ETHICAL CONFLICTS

Conflicting loyalties, fear of failure, and/or the fear of being fired put our ethical values on the line. How would you respond to each of the following situations? Be honest!

Would you:

	YES	NO
—Alter a financial report at your boss's direction?	☐	☐
—Protect a friend and co-worker whose drinking is causing productivity problems in your unit?	☐	☐
—Take credit for work on a report that was prepared by someone else?	☐	☐
—Put off correcting a safety situation because the cost will decrease your division's profitability?	☐	☐
—Change a performance appraisal to reflect more positively on an individual whose advancement is important to your supervisor?	☐	☐

Take a few minutes to think about specific ethical conflicts you face on your job. What things would you not do, even at the risk of being fired? I would refuse to:

_____

_____

_____

_____

ETHICAL ATTITUDES

The way you deal with ethical situations reflects your background, training, and personal style. Check the box that best describes your attitude.

☐ I believe that as long as I am working for this organization I should follow its policies and carry out the assignments as given to me by my superiors. I've spent several years doing my job and the company has been good to me. If people don't like something that is asked of them, they should get out and go to work somewhere else.

☐ I've always worked with the idea that you should look out for yourself and not get involved in other people's problems. I believe it works out best this way in the long run. I've got my job to take care of and if I do it well, it will benefit not only me, but the company, too. The main thing is to get my job done, let other people get their job done, and not worry too much about all the rules.

☐ I know that I need a job to make money. I also know that the company has to make a profit, but I think I can be sensitive to what is right and wrong and still do a good job. In fact, if I don't act in an ethical way, in the long run it could damage not only my integrity but also that of the company.

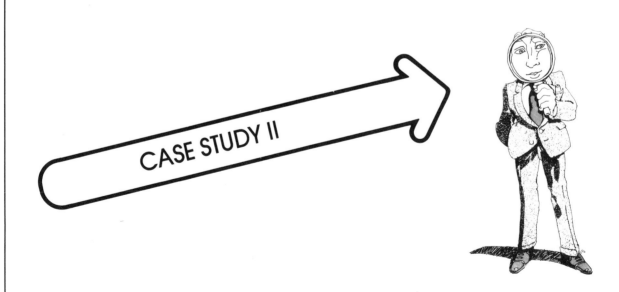

CASE STUDY II

CASE STUDY II

The Dilemma at the Build Big Company

Build Big Company is in stiff competition for the dwindling amount of prime residential building land available near a fast-growing urban area. Although the law of supply and demand has driven house prices to astronomical heights, costs of building have kept rapid pace, and profit margins for *Build Big* are narrow.

A thicket of local building regulations, environmental impact reports, developer fees and permits complicate the process, but they have also provided opportunities for special ''arrangements'' with two discreet county officials who will expedite transactions for an added gratuity. It's common practice with some of *Build Big's* competitors.

Build Big's President, J.B., has wrestled with the question of gratuities for some time. There is increasing legal risk in the situation. Also, J.B. has prided himself through the years for being totally honest. Now the competition has never been tougher, and J.B. is starting to suffer economically because his projects move slower than those of his competitors.

J.B. calls in Sam, who has responsibility for obtaining the necessary permits. ''We need to stay competitive,'' says J.B., ''We've got nearly 250 people on the payroll, and that's a lot of jobs to lose if we can't compete. See who you can talk to, Sam. I don't care what you need to do to get the permits approved...just do it.''

How do you think Sam should respond?

_____

_____

_____

_____

_____

_____

_____

_____

Check your ideas with the author's on page 66.

PART III
ETHICAL CONSIDERATIONS
IN TRANSACTIONS
WITH EMPLOYEES

IDENTIFYING ETHICAL CONCERNS IN EMPLOYEE TRANSACTIONS

Supervisors and managers are continually involved with employees and prospective employees. They are responsible for numerous decisions that affect the self-esteem, personal growth, morale, and economic well-being of those they manage. Are there ethical overtones in these decisions? In the list below, check those transactions you feel involve ethics.

☐ 1. Selecting new employees

☐ 2. Awarding merit increases

☐ 3. Setting goals and performance standards

☐ 4. Evaluating performance

☐ 5. Giving performance feedback

☐ 6. Disciplining

☐ 7. Selecting personnel for promotion

☐ 8. Terminating employee services

☐ 9. Communicating

☐ 10. Supporting employee ideas and efforts

☐ 11. Delegating work

☐ 12. Arranging training and development opportunities

☐ 13. Providing healthful, safe working conditions

☐ 14. Granting time off with or without pay

If you checked all the above items, you are very sensitive to the part ethics play in decisions involving the needs of employees as they relate to the organization and that require you to differentiate between people.

If you checked only twelve of the items, you need to think seriously about what you are doing and your impact upon the well being of individuals and the organization. If you checked less than ten, some very serious thought is needed on your part and you are urged to discuss the ethics of these issues with other managers as well as concentrating on the content of this book.

ETHICAL IMPLICATIONS IN CHOOSING BETWEEN PEOPLE

Managers continually choose between people when making decisions such as which job seeker to hire, which employee to promote, or which employee to lay off. These decisions are especially difficult when they concern long-term employees, people with personal problems, older workers, minorities or people with marginal skills in an increasingly technical business environment.

Managers cannot help being torn by conflicting personal interests and biases, loyalties to individuals, friendships, organizational needs, the impact on the well-being of the employee, and, in some cases, the implications for his or her own status in the organization.

An ethical outcome requires focusing objectively on the issues at hand. The next page suggests how this can be accomplished.

MANAGERS WHO CONSISTENTLY MAKE ETHICALLY SOUND DECISIONS DO SO ONLY AFTER WRESTLING OBJECTIVELY WITH THE ISSUES.

IMPROVE YOUR OBJECTIVITY

CHOOSING BETWEEN PEOPLE

Managers will find it helpful to ask themselves a variety of questions when faced with the task of choosing between people. The questions should be designed to reveal the real issues, as well as their feelings toward them and the people involved.

Objectivity is the desired goal in making such decisions, but the temptation is often great to slide through with as little personal pain as possible. Resist this temptation because the issues deserve your profound attention and honest consideration.

The following questions are designed to promote objectivity. Check those you already ask and place an X by those you will ask in the future.

☐ 1. Am I biased toward the employee for any reason?

☐ 2. Am I evaluating demonstrated skills bona fide against job requirements?

☐ 3. Am I being overly influenced one way or the other by irrelevant or surface characteristics?

☐ 4. Am I being pushed in a direction not of my choice by someone else?

☐ 5. Am I measuring all people against the same criteria?

☐ 6. Is age or salary level influencing my thinking more than it should?

☐ 7. Am I really analyzing the important elements of this transaction or am I simply following a past practice that should be tested?

☐ 8. Will the final decision be in the best interest of the individual, the organization and myself?

☐ 9. Would I be willing to have my decision criteria applied to me under similar circumstances?

Rationalization is a powerful force we often use to comfort ourselves after making poor decisions. NEVER LET PERSONAL BIASES OVERWHELM YOUR OBJECTIVITY OR SENSE OF FAIRNESS!

ETHICS AND PERFORMANCE APPRAISAL

Managers sometimes resist doing performance appraisals on the grounds they do not want to be judge and jury with respect to an employee's career. Some feel positive feedback will cause employees to let down. Others think that negative feedback is demoralizing, demeaning, and perhaps unethical, so they often give employees better performance appraisals than they deserve. Still others see performance appraisals as a way to cut people down or keep them under their thumb. In all these cases, the managers' ethics must be questioned.

Failing to be honest with employees about their performance is a form of deceit that is damaging to the employee, the organization, and the manager. Managers who practice this deceit either do not know how to evaluate employees properly or simply do not take a sincere interest in their performance.

Managers who follow correct performance evaluation and feedback procedures create an environment in which there are no surprises, and employees have the opportunity to correct deficiences and grow. Under such circumstances ethics become a matter of honesty and fairness in dealing with issues both the manager and the employee understand.

Research reveals that more than half the professional and clerical employees working today do not understand how their work is evaluated. If this could be true of your employees, familiarize them with the process now and tell new employees when they begin work how they will be evaluated. To do otherwise may well be unethical.

CASE STUDY III

The Dance Of The Lemons

When Gregory Samuels joined the Alpha Corporation, he sat down with Linda Jensen, the senior executive to whom he reported, to learn the goals of the organization, and to find out as specifically as possible what was expected of him. As the discussion progressed, Gregory became increasingly ill at ease. Ms. Jensen seemed reluctant to talk in specifics, and avoided sharing confidential information pertinent to Gregory's position.

As the discussion progressed and Gregory's frustration grew, he asked Ms. Jensen about the new assignment his predecessor had been given. "Oh," Ms. Jensen said with a sly grin, "he has joined the Dance of the Lemons." "What do you mean?" asked Gregory. "Well," said Ms. Jensen, "he was not performing effectively, so we moved him to another assignment." "Will he do better there?" asked Gregory. "Who knows?" said Ms. Jensen "but at least he's out of my hair."

"Was there any particular reason why you assigned him to another position, rather than terminate him?" Gregory asked. "Oh, we seldom terminate senior employees, we just move them around the organization hoping we will find a place they will fit. All of us know these moves happen—we call it the Dance of the Lemons."

Sixty days later, after having located another position, Gregory resigned.

Why do you think Gregory resigned?

_____

_____

What would you have done under similar circumstances?

_____

_____

Does this case involve managerial ethics? Why or why not?

_____

_____

See page 67 for the author's response.

IMPROVE YOUR ETHICAL BATTING AVERAGE

You can be successful at performance appraisal and have a clear conscience, or be a miserable failure filled with doubt and remorse. Note the factors that make the difference below.

SUCCESSFUL APPRAISERS	MISERABLE FAILURES
Leaders who engage in mutual goal setting and open communication.	Those who establish arbitrary, unilateral performance goals or standards. They may or may not communicate them to employees.
Leaders who establish clear, measurable expectations and provide a climate conducive to success.	Those who have not thought through what they expect or don't know how to measure success, thereby creating a threatening atmosphere in which to work.
Leaders who ask questions, listen carefully and appreciate and use the ideas of others.	Those who never seek the ideas of others or listen, yet have a solution for everyone else's problems.
Leaders who publicly recognize positive performance and privately correct improper performance when it occurs.	Those who spend too much time looking for things that are wrong and too little looking for things that are right.
Leaders who give honest feedback on performance against mutually understood goals.	Those who accept substandard performance or misrepresent it in providing feedback.
Leaders who follow through on their commitments.	Those who do not take their commitments seriously.

> An ethical performance appraisal is a fair and honest assessment of performance against mutually established and understood goals and standards that leaves both parties feeling they have gained something.

ETHICS AND COMMUNICATION WITH EMPLOYEES

When employees discuss how trust is built in work groups, they stress the importance of open and honest communication. They refer to this kind of communication as "leveling," or "telling it like it is."

Employees who make productivity gains often attribute much of their achievement to being well-informed about goals, standards, time tables, costs and other elements or objectives of assigned tasks. Supervisors who withhold information, whether inadvertently or intentionally, impede employee efforts and compromise the progress or quality of their work.

There is considerable evidence that individuals communicate better with people they like than with those they dislike or about whom they are neutral. If a manager spends more time with employees they like and talk with them more, tell them more, and are more open to their questions, these favored few have an advantage over others. Favoritism of any kind places employees on unequal footing and potentially damages the work group, the organization and the supervisor.

Managers wanting to be more fair and open in their communication should ask themselves these questions frequently:

What do employees working for me *need* to know?

What do employees working for me *want* to know?

How do I provide it?

When do I get someone else to provide it?

ETHICAL APPROACHES TO MAINTAINING DISCIPLINE

It is a fundamental concept in organizations that managers are responsible for maintaining discipline among the employees they supervise. All too often, however, discipline is misunderstood, or ignored. Many managers take little corrective action unless there is a serious breach of conduct. Consequently, unless managers understand their roles relative to discipline, they are apt to either under- or over-react. Either reaction has ethical connotations because the results of an inappropriate reaction can have negative consequences for managers, employees and the organization. These consequences often take the form of grievances, complaints of discrimination, law suits, loss of income, termination, lowered productivity, or general unrest or unhappiness.

A well-disciplined work group is one that operates like a team. It works productively while adhering to all *necessary* rules and regulations. A manager who wishes to have such a group must insure all employees are properly trained and motivated to attain the standards of performance desired.

It is helpful to remember the word "discipline" comes from the same root as the word "disciple" and means "to teach so as to mold." Unfortunately, many managers never learn the "teaching and molding" aspects of discipline, and think of it instead as punishment or a reprimand. It is in the best interest of everyone to accentuate the positive when approaching discipline because in most instances this approach reduces or eliminates the need for negative actions.

You can accentuate the positive by doing essentially what all good coaches do:

1. Make sure your players know the standards of performance desired.

2. Teach them how to attain standards.

3. Encourage them as they progress in the direction desired.

4. Compliment them when they attain standards and continue to reinforce positive performance periodically.

DISCIPLINARY GUIDELINES

Unfortunately, even the best manager will, at some point, have an employee who does not follow the rules. Consequently, this manager, like a coach, will have to counsel the player. This may take the form of training, a warning, or reprimand. In serious cases it can involve suspension or discharge.

Managers can take action ethically by adhering to the following guidelines. Rate yourself on how well you handle each.

	HIGH			LOW	
1. I determine whether the employee has been warned and understands the consequences of such conduct.	5	4	3	2	1
2. I assure myself the order or rule violated is reasonably related to safe, ethical, legal or efficient operations.	5	4	3	2	1
3. I make sure disciplinary action is not taken until a complete investigation has been completed.	5	4	3	2	1
4. I make every effort to assure the investigation is fair, objective and includes the employee's input.	5	4	3	2	1
5. I analyze the evidence carefully to determine whether it provides substantial proof of guilt.	5	4	3	2	1
6. I check to see if the rules or orders violated have been consistently enforced in the past.	5	4	3	2	1
7. I make sure the penalty is reasonably related to the seriousness of the offense, and is applied even-handedly and without discrimination.	5	4	3	2	1

TOTAL _____

If you scored 28 or above you seem to be on target in administering discipline. If you scored between 21 and 27 you have the right idea but need to work harder in those areas where your score is 3 or lower. If you scored under 21 you need to reexamine your approach to discipline and seek appropriate training.

ADMINISTERING REWARD SYSTEMS

Many incentive systems have been designed by organizations wanting to reward their employees for above-average performance. Unfortunately, these systems often fall prey to unethical administrative practices. If this happens, employees are penalized and the intent of the process is destroyed.

Managers charged with the administration of merit and bonus budgets, for example, often are unwilling to differentiate between employees on the basis of performance. They simply divide rewards equally, or nearly so, among performers who may range from inadequate to outstanding. When this happens they end up reinforcing poor performance while penalizing superior work.

Some managers are afraid if they recognize good performance one year, they are locked into giving similar recognition next year, earned or not. Some also feel it is necessary to give an adequate performer a raise every year. Still others feel giving a substandard performer an increase might motivate better performance. Then, of course, there are a few who want to reward only their friends. All of the above approaches are seriously flawed, and filled with ethical pitfalls.

Incentive systems are designed to reward people on the basis of performance and their overall contribution to the organization. Managers must be honest. They must understand the work being performed and be able to differentiate clearly between levels of performance by individuals. They must also have some personal convictions about what is right and wrong, as well as the courage to stand behind their decisions. You will find some guidance for doing this on the next page.

GUIDELINES FOR THE ETHICAL ADMINISTRATION OF REWARD SYSTEMS

Managers wanting to review how objective they are in administrating reward systems can do so on the rating scale below. Circle the number that best represents you. A 5 is a perfect score on each item.

WHEN I ADMINISTER REWARD SYSTEMS:

	HIGH			LOW	
1. I lay ground work by insuring there is mutual understanding with each employee about what is expected in terms of performance.	5	4	3	2	1
2. I update job descriptions as changes occur and insist that the salary grades of my employees remain appropriate to their positions.	5	4	3	2	1
3. I consistently monitor performance against expectations and give all employees appropriate feedback.	5	4	3	2	1
4. I am alert for both superior or inferior performance as related to goals and standards.	5	4	3	2	1
5. I note, and communicate to others, employee efforts to develop and increase their potential.	5	4	3	2	1
6. I refuse to let nonperformance factors like friendship, race, religion, family background, sex, or age influence my decisions.	5	4	3	2	1
7. I test my decisions to be sure they are based on facts and not just assumptions or impressions.	5	4	3	2	1
8. I make my decisions on objective data and push aside any unwillingness to help my employees face reality.	5	4	3	2	1
9. When I observe others who are unethical in distributing awards, I resist the same impulse in myself.	5	4	3	2	1
10. I strive to maintain equity between employees and am prepared to justify with facts my decisions to anyone.	5	4	3	2	1

TOTAL _____

A score below 40 suggests you need to do some hard work to improve the ethical administration of your reward systems.

PART IV
ETHICAL CONSIDERATIONS
IN TRANSACTIONS WITH
YOUR BOSS

HMMMMM . . . .

SOURCES OF ETHICAL CONCERNS IN TRANSACTIONS WITH THE BOSS

Every manager has a manager. The two frequently interact in pursuing the best interests of their organization. The issues they are involved with are numerous, varied, and often complex. Often ethical considerations are involved. In some cases managers will address and resolve ethical issues together. In other cases they will disagree on what to do. Sometimes a manager and his or her boss will assign widely differing degrees of importance to an issue and its possible outcome.

In the list below, identify situations you know or believe have definite ethical overtones.

☐   1. Goal setting

☐   2. Communicating

☐   3. Following orders

☐   4. Supporting actions and decisions

☐   5. Establishing and administering policies

☐   6. Providing healthy and safe working conditions

☐   7. Solving problems

☐   8. Selecting employees

☐   9. Rewarding employees

☐ 10. Disciplining employees

☐ 11. Evaluating employees

☐ 12. Delegating tasks

☐ 13. Training employees

☐ 14. Breaking promises

☐ 15. Using employee ideas

If you checked all the above situations you are very much aware of the ethical potential in transactions with your boss. If you checked 12 or less, you need to give more thought to this aspect of your relationship, and work toward dealing with ethical issues appropriately and directly.

FOLLOWING ORDERS AND DIRECTIVES FROM ABOVE

Managers are expected to follow orders from above and normally do so with a minimum of questions or concerns. They usually have an opportunity to explore alternatives, and comment on any aspect of the directive they feel may be inappropriate or improper. When they can demonstrate the merits of their concern, they are often successful in obtaining changes or modifications.

On occasion, an order from above might not only affect employees, customers and the general public negatively, but might also be unethical. A manager who passes on this order may not have considered the ethics involved, or may not care about the consequences. It is also possible the originator of the directive left the manager no choice in the matter.

This is an especially difficult problem for managers who value ethics and have genuine concern for the well-being of those affected, as well as for the reputation of the organization. It is a time when the manager has to examine personal values carefully and weigh them against the possible consequences of challenging the directive.

WHEN ETHICS ARE INVOLVED, THIS IS NEVER THE BEST COURSE OF ACTION...EVEN WITH A TOUGH BOSS.

JUST DO IT!

FOLLOWING ORDERS (Continued)

You may decide a challenge is imperative. Such a choice is yours alone to make. A decision to challenge, no matter how tactfully, has the potential to result in personal repercussions. A decision to do otherwise, however, may be the first step to support and carry out ethically questionable decisions that will ultimately lower your self-respect and personal credibility. It is a choice you must make based on your value system and judgment. It is never a good idea to support a policy that compromises your integrity or self-respect.

> When considering whether or not to challenge a directive or a situation you consider unethical, remember that such challenges are often successful when you can suggest a better alternative.

CASE STUDY IV

CASE STUDY IV

Just A Modest Change In The Records

Jenny Larson was a senior human resources executive reporting to the Vice President of Employee Relations, of a major company when this incident occured. One of her responsibilities was administering the psychological assessment program for, and maintaining the assessment profiles on, all senior executives.

The Executive Committee of the Board of Directors asked for a summary profile on each senior executive for succession planning purposes. Jenny felt that to prevent misinterpretation these summaries should be prepared by the consulting firm that had done the original assessments, and therefore she instructed them to do so.

The consulting firm completed the summaries as instructed and forwarded them to the Vice President of Employee Relations, for review. He then passed them along to Jenny, who was to prepare the final compilation for the Executive Committee. The next week several revised summaries came from the Vice President. He had made significant changes to the consultants' summaries. On one summary, for example, the Vice President had changed ''promotable'' to ''not promotable.'' Jenny was appalled at the changes, and concerned about what to do. The modifications violated her sense of ethics, but she was afraid if she questioned them, she would place her job and her future in jeopardy. The more she thought about it, the more concerned she became. Was it possible someone above the Vice President level had requested these changes?

What would you have done if you were Jenny? Why?

_____

_____

_____

_____

What consequences would you have expected?

_____

_____

_____

_____

Turn to page 68 for the authors comments.

SUPPORTING AND COMMUNICATING

Few people advance very far in an organization without having found a way to harmonize their thoughts and actions with those of the manager to whom they report. Doing so requires effort, and often some compromise. It should never require sacrificing personal integrity.

Mutual confidence is central to a good supervisor/employee relationship and must be earned by both parties. As the subordinate manager, you have an obligation to keep your boss informed of decisions and developments in your operations that he or she needs to know in order to make good decisions. This calls for timely communication and accurate reporting. It should not require the betrayal of confidences existing between you, your own subordinates, and your peers.

Improve your upward communication significantly by reflecting on the following questions and discussing each with your boss. Then follow through and provide the information as determined by your meeting.

1. What information should I pass on to satisfy my bosses need to know and to facilitate decision making.

2. How should it be conveyed?

3. How often is it required?

ASSESS YOUR SUPPORT AND UPWARD COMMUNICATION SKILLS

Answer the following True/False questions.

| TRUE | FALSE |

_____ _____ 1. Communicating employee ideas up the line with appropriate credit is important to my boss and fair to my employees.

_____ _____ 2. Knocking my boss in discussions with employees and peers is a good practice and will improve my image.

_____ _____ 3. There is no harm in telling the boss a job is finished if it makes him or her happy and completion is only hours away.

_____ _____ 4. It is important to give my boss accurate feedback about how employees view the organization, but naming names can be unethical.

_____ _____ 5. If I frequently find it difficult to support my boss, I would be wise to seek a transfer or another position elsewhere.

_____ _____ 6. When a project is falling seriously behind schedule or is about to fail, my boss should be advised immediately.

_____ _____ 7. There is little reason to inform my boss when an employee excels at a task as long as I reward that employee properly.

_____ _____ 8. It is inappropriate for me to share my boss's confidences with anyone else.

_____ _____ 9. It's O.K. to agree to goals, standards, and time tables I know cannot be met if they seem important to the boss.

_____ _____ 10. Telling my boss that I strongly suspect one of my employees is sexually harassing another would be a breach of ethics.

_____ _____ 11. Making up achievements to justify higher raises for my employees will help them and make me and my boss look good.

_____ _____ 12. It's a good idea to overstate my case when selling an idea to the boss.

_____ _____ 13. The boss will reward my delaying for as long as possible, expenditures for needed health and safety improvements.

_____ _____ 14. My boss won't mind if I attribute my criticism of the work habits of my employees to him or her.

_____ _____ 15. It's O.K. to have genuine respect for my boss and to let it be known.

Turn the page to check your answers.

ANSWERS

ASSESS YOUR SUPPORT AND UPWARD COMMUNICATION SKILLS

1. TRUE   It is also critical to your personal success!

2. FALSE   It is never a good idea to criticize your boss to others. It is damaging to morale, productivity and your reputation. If you have a problem with him or her, talk it over and strive for better understanding.

3. FALSE   Making the boss happy is not the primary criterion in reporting results. Honesty and accuracy are much more important in the long run.

4. TRUE   Good managers very seldom ask a subordinate to divulge the source of personal confidences because doing so will cut off the flow of important information.

5. TRUE   If you cannot support your boss most of the time, you are of little value to the boss or yourself. If you can't work it out, get out!

6. TRUE   Your boss may need to advise others. It's also dishonest!

7. FALSE   The boss should always be kept aware of those who excel consistently, or even occasionally, so that he or she can also recognize their effort and support your efforts to reward them.

8. TRUE   Sharing confidences is a sign of trust. Don't risk losing it.

9. FALSE   Giving the boss false expectations is never acceptable.

10. FALSE   This could have critical consequences and should not come as a surprise to your boss. He or she should also know what you are doing about the situation.

11. FALSE   Misrepresentation is never acceptable.

12. FALSE   The risks of doing so are high—are you prepared to pay the price?

13. FALSE   A good boss will have you on the carpet for this.

14. FALSE   If you have to attribute your criticism of an employee to someone else, you don't show much promise for the future.

15. TRUE   And don't you forget it!

TEN ETHICAL MISTAKES TO AVOID

Check those mistakes you intend to avoid in dealing with your boss. I will avoid:

☐ 1. Lying or in any way misrepresenting the facts about the activities I direct.

☐ 2. Blaming my boss for my personal mistakes or those of my employees.

☐ 3. Divulging personal or confidential information to peers, senior managers, employees, customers, competitors, or the general public.

☐ 4. Permitting, or failing to report, violations of any federal, state, or municipal laws or regulations.

☐ 5. Protecting substandard performers from corrective discipline or termination.

☐ 6. Condoning or failing to report the theft or misuse of company property.

☐ 7. Supressing greivances and complaints.

☐ 8. Covering up on-the-job accidents and failing to report health and safety hazards.

☐ 9. Ignoring or violating the boss's commitments to employees.

☐ 10. Passing on employee ideas as my own.

PART V
ETHICAL CONSIDERATIONS
IN TRANSACTIONS
WITH PEERS

ETHICAL ISSUES IN PEER TRANSACTIONS

Managers are often interdependent and have many contacts with their peers. Mutual cooperation and trust are essential aspects of peer relationships and are usually earned over a period of time. Ethics often play a significant role in the success or failure of these relationships and need to be tended carefully.

In the list of transactions below, check those you either know from experience, or strongly sense, have ethical overtones.

☐ 1. Transferring employees between groups

☐ 2. Sharing facilities, tools or equipment

☐ 3. Meeting shared deadlines

☐ 4. Evaluating individuals or groups

☐ 5. Managing change

☐ 6. Communicating across organizational lines

☐ 7. Taking credit for another's accomplishments

☐ 8. Leaving work for the next shift

☐ 9. Disrupting others through actions you take

☐ 10. Supporting the ideas, opinions and work of others

☐ 11. Administering policy and procedure

☐ 12. Determining action that will be mutually beneficial

☐ 13. Maintaining salary equity between individuals and groups

☐ 14. Identifying mutual objectives

☐ 15. Solving mutual problems

☐ 16. Protecting confidences

☐ 17. Granting special privileges

☐ 18. Maintaining discipline even when it involves peers

☐ 19. Maintaining a safe environment

☐ 20. Eliminating bias and prejudice throughout the organization

---

If you checked 15 or more items, you seem aware of the ethical implications of your interaction with peers. If you checked less than 12, it's time to rethink your relationship with and your impact on your peers.

SUPPORTING AND COMMUNICATING WITH PEERS

Managers who do not relate well with peers and other associates usually have a difficult time accomplishing their goals and moving up in the organization. The interdependence of departments requires cooperation, which is best achieved by good communication and concern for the well-being of others.

Maintaining a team spirit between peers and work groups is difficult under the best of circumstances. When individuals try to take advantage of others, or to make them look bad, everyone loses.

Peer relationships require a win/win attitude on the part of all concerned. Do you have one? In the box below, check the win/win characteristics you consistently practice.

☐ 1. I realize that when I win and everyone else loses there will come a day of retribution. I prefer the shared pleasure of everyone getting what they need.

☐ 2. I am genuinely interested in meeting the needs and contributing to the success of my peers and support them accordingly.

☐ 3. I am flexible in my approach to solving mutual problems, and am willing to make some concessions to satisfy others' needs as well as my own.

☐ 4. I am cooperative rather than contentious.

☐ 5. I fully understand that to achieve what my group wants, we may have to give up something.

Productive relationships depend on open communication, so managers must carefully consider the needs of peers, as well as those of superiors and employees, if *all* the work of the organization is to be done efficiently. The following questions may help you decide when and what you need to communicate.

—What groups depend on me for information?
—What do they need to know?
—When do they need to know it?
—How do I provide it?

COLLABORATION—A BENEFICIAL AND ETHICAL TOOL

Competition between managers and between work groups sometimes gets out of hand. When it does, questionable practices are often employed to get ahead, or to make the other party look bad. Good ethics are often suspended and the organization suffers.

Collaboration is a much better management tool. Better yet, it's ethical. In the list below, check the benefits of collaboration that are important to you. I believe:

☐ Collaboration builds an awareness of interdependence. When people recognize the benefits of helping one another, they are more likely to work together to accomplish common goals. The effort is non-threatening.

☐ When people work together they stimulate each other to higher levels of achievement. Fresh ideas are generated and tested, and productivity increases.

☐ Collaboration builds and reinforces recognition and mutual support. People can see the result of their effort, and the efforts of others, in their achievements.

☐ Collaboration leads to a commitment to accomplish organizational goals. People gain personal power, in the form of confidence, when they know others share their views and are acting in concert with them.

The benefits of collaboration make it easy to understand why managers who can make it happen are considered leaders. Collaboration can be encouraged and supported in the following ways. Check those you plan to use.

☐ Identify areas of interdependence that make collaboration appropriate. Involve peers in planning and problem solving to help them identify where collaboration is needed.

☐ Keep the lines of communication open between everyone involved in a problem, project or course of action.

☐ Secure positive recognition for those who participate in collaborative efforts.

CONSTRUCTIVE PROBLEM SOLVING

All too often results are poor when peers are brought together to solve problems. Reasons include concern about turf, internal politics, jealousy and/or sacred cows. Individual ethics are often severly tested.

Much better results are obtained when a conscious decision is made to use sound group processes. When participants commit themselves to finding the best possible solution, rather than to imposing their view exclusively sound results can be expected. Open communication encourages employees to challenge and test the usefulness of ideas in solving problems. The following conditions support effective problem solving. Check ☑ those you already use and place an ☒ by those you will add in the future.

1. Participants readily contribute ideas and listen to the contributions of others.

2. Conflicts arising from different points of view are considered helpful and are resolved constructively.

3. Participants feel free to challenge suggestions they believe are unsupported by the facts or logic, but avoid arguing just to have their way.

4. Poor solutions are not supported just for the sake of harmony or agreement.

5. Differences of opinion are discussed and resolved. Coin tossing, averaging, majority vote, and similar cop-outs are avoided when making a decision.

6. Every participant strives to make the problem-solving process efficient and is careful to facilitate, rather than hinder, discussion.

7. Participants encourage and support co-workers who may be reluctant to offer ideas.

8. Participants understand the value of time and work at eliminating extraneous or repetitious discussion.

BE A PART OF THE SOLUTION—NOT PART OF THE PROBLEM!

CASE STUDY V

The Dueling Managers

Peter Lee, Operations Manager, and Jan Nelson, Maintenance Manager, both report to Harry Hart, General Manager of Turbo Chemicals. Peter and Jan are about the same age, well-educated and have extensive experience in their respective fields. It would be expected that these two individuals would complement each other and be the answer to every general manager's prayer. Unfortunately, that is not the case.

For some reason, Peter and Jan find it necessary to challenge each other's decisions and ideas anytime they have a mutual problem to solve, and they argue constantly in staff meetings. Recently Jan began to talk to peers in an effort to get them on her side. Peter learning of this, went to Harry Hart and demanded that he call Jan in and tell her to stop. Peter didn't realize Harry Hart was aware of what was happening. Nor did he know Harry had just learned that Peter had deliberately changed a unit turnaround schedule so that it would fall during a period when the maintenance department already had a peak workload.

The matter has been further complicated by the fact that the employees of the two managers have taken sides and joined the fray. Productive work has come to a standstill.

What are the ethics involved in this case?

_____

_____

How would you proceed if you were Harry Hart?

_____

_____

_____

_____

Turn to page 69 for the author's comments.

PART VI
SOLVING ETHICAL PROBLEMS

AN ORGANIZED APPROACH

In recent years it has been popular to regard managers as decision makers and problem solvers. The effective manager is often thought of as one who makes quick decisions in a variety of areas.

Actually, it is not essential that managers make a stream of fast decisions about a multitude of issues. It is more important that they make a few, right decisions in crucial areas of their responsibility.

The best way to solve problems at any management level is to make sure that most problems that are inconsequential never get to this level. Reducing the total number of problems a manager has to solve personally frees enough time for that person to handle crucial problems that demand prudent judgment. This includes ethical problems.

Ethical problems can be solved just like any others. When a problem you should solve or a decision you should make presents itself, approach it in an organized, systematic way. The guidelines presented in the next few pages are suggested for solving ethical problems.

SIMPLY OVERLOOKING THE ETHICAL IMPLICATIONS OF AN ISSUE IS ONE OF THE MAJOR CAUSES OF ETHICAL FAILURES!

SOLVING ETHICAL PROBLEMS: THE TEN STEP METHOD

STEP ONE—DEFINE THE PROBLEM

Intricate problems, with a jumble of facts from a variety of sources, confront managers. Often the apparent problem is only a symptom of the actual one.

For instance: Will drug tests prevent the sale and use of drugs on the job? Will they improve productivity without upsetting and alienating non-users, who will also be required to take the tests?

Is it fair to require employees to take the tests?

Are the tests reliable?

Do employees have the right to refuse to take the tests?

Would you fire a long term, loyal, and productive employee who refused to take the tests?

STEP TWO—IS IT AN ETHICAL PROBLEM OR A STRAIGHT FORWARD BUSINESS DECISION?

If issues like personal rights, fairness, equity, honesty, and morality surface, it's an ethical problem and should be treated accordingly. Drug testing is an ethical problem.

STEP THREE—IDENTIFY THOSE ELEMENTS OF THE PROBLEM THAT ARE ETHICAL CONCERNS.

Are drug tests O.K. if they are voluntary?

If the drug tests result in signs of drug abuse, but the employee is always productive and never a hazard, can you or should you fire him or her?

SOLVING ETHICAL PROBLEMS
(Continued)

> **STEP FOUR**—IS THE PROBLEM A CASE OF DIFFERING OPINIONS, A CONFLICT OF INTEREST, OR A QUESTION OF RIGHTS AND FAIRNESS?

Do disputed drug tests indicate a difference of opinion between management and employees? Do they violate an individual's right to privacy?

> **STEP FIVE**—IS IT A PERSONAL PROBLEM, A COMPANY PROBLEM, AN INDUSTRY PROBLEM, OR A CULTURAL PROBLEM?

Drug testing fits all these categories.

> **STEP SIX**—WHO IS AFFECTED?

In the case of drug testing, all employees (and their families), supervisors, and managers are affected.

> **STEP SEVEN**—IS SPECIAL HELP NEEDED?

Experts in the field of drug abuse, testing, human resources management, and human behavior may be helpful in establishing an appropriate program or otherwise solving the problem.

SOLVING ETHICAL PROBLEMS
(Continued)

STEP EIGHT—WHAT ARE THE ALTERNATIVE SOLUTIONS?

Every problem has a number of alternative solutions. They must first be identified, then evaluated. Which is the best solution? Will there be positive, negative, or neutral side effects?

Will mandatory drug tests stop drug abuse and improve job performance, or will employees be alienated to the extent performance suffers even more?

Will voluntary testing solve the performance problem without angering employees?

Will terminating employees for documented substandard performance resolve the primary issue?

STEP NINE—ARE THE PROPOSED SOLUTIONS LEGAL, MORAL, CULTURALLY ACCEPTABLE, AND IN KEEPING WITH GOOD BUSINESS PRACTICE? DOES THE SOLUTION SUPPORT THE IMAGE YOU AND THE ORGANIZATION WISH TO HAVE WITH EMPLOYEES, CUSTOMERS, COMPETITORS, AND THE GENERAL PUBLIC?

Mandatory drug testing is still very controversial. Documented efforts to constructively improve performance when it falls below established standards is an accepted practice. It either brings performance up to standards or eliminates the poor performer from the organization.

STEP TEN—CAN THE SOLUTION BE IMPLEMENTED AT REASONABLE COST, WITH A MINIMUM OF DISRUPTION AND WITH A HIGH DEGREE OF PROBABLE SUCCESS?

Testing is expensive in terms of both dollars and morale and is often disruptive. Bringing performance up to standards is hard work and requires well-trained managers, but it should be ongoing in any organization that wants to succeed.

CASE STUDY VI

Is Process Insurance Enough?

The maintenance, operations, and safety managers of a large chemical company met with the plant manager to discuss safety features that should be designed into the construction of a new process unit for the manufacture of a highly volatile new chemical product. It would be a significant addition to the plant and employ four people per shift.

The safety features under consideration covered all aspects of risk. In total, they would be extremely expensive to install and maintain. The group deliberated a long time over the probabilities of explosion or fire. They finally agreed that all of the safety devices recommended would prevent the possible hazards, but they were greatly concerned about the cost. Finally, one member of the group said, "Look, it's just not cost-effective to spend the money. What do we have to lose? Our insurance will fully reimburse us for product loss if the unit malfunctions and blows up. It is such a remote possibility that it doesn't make sense to spend the money."

How would you have responded if you had been a member of this group?

_____

_____

_____

_____

_____

_____

_____

_____

_____

_____

_____

_____

_____

_____

Turn to page 70 for the author's comments.

PART VII
REVIEW AND SUGGESTIONS
FOR THE FUTURE

THIS IS A GOOD TIME TO TAKE A MOMENT TO REFLECT ON WHAT YOU HAVE READ. COMPLETING THE EXERCISE ON THE NEXT PAGE WILL HELP STIMULATE YOUR THINKING.

READING REVIEW

Answer the following true/false questions.

TRUE	FALSE

_____ _____ 1. Ethics are of concern only to senior managers.

_____ _____ 2. Ethical considerations are vital elements in choosing between people.

_____ _____ 3. Performance appraisals require good standards, hard work and open communication between employee and manager.

_____ _____ 4. The primary consideration in granting this year's merit increases and bonuses is the amount given last year.

_____ _____ 5. It's completely ethical to violate the rights of others if it gets you what you want.

_____ _____ 6. If you can't support and endorse your boss, it's time to find another.

_____ _____ 7. Employees will generally support a boss who cuts ethical corners.

_____ _____ 8. Creating conflict with your peers and involving your employees in interdepartmental disputes is good, competitive fun.

_____ _____ 9. If one of your co-workers seems to be better regarded than yourself, be sure to point up his or her shortcomings.

_____ _____ 10. Most of us have had little exposure to ethical role models or sound ethical principles.

READING REVIEW (Continued)

TRUE	FALSE

_____   _____   11. Ethical problems can be solved using sound problem-solving techniques.

_____   _____   12. Following the boss's direct orders is a good way to avoid making ethical errors.

_____   _____   13. Collaboration with your peers is healthy and ethical when it is done for the right reasons.

_____   _____   14. Safety and health are not ethical decisions. They are strictly financial decisions.

_____   _____   15. Since you're the boss, you can ethically fire an employee for any reason you choose.

_____   _____   16. Managers are often role models for their subordinates.

Check your answers with the authors' answers on the next page.

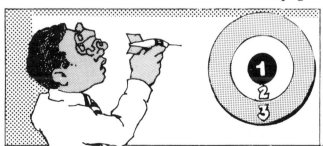

NEVER LEAVE ETHICS TO CHANCE!

ANSWERS
READING REVIEW

1. FALSE Ethics are everyone's concern!

2. TRUE   Discrimination is unethical and in many cases unlawful.

3. TRUE   Without these elements you might just as well forget appraisals.

4. FALSE Performance should be the primary criterion.

5. FALSE Violating the rights of others is never ethical.

6. TRUE   Do it now!

7. FALSE It makes them very uncomfortable and they lose self-respect.

8. FALSE It is seldom fun and never productive. Find a positive basis for competition.

9. FALSE Improve your own performance instead.

10. FALSE See Part II.

11. TRUE   It takes time, but the results are worth it.

12. FALSE Bosses make ethical mistakes too. Try to suggest a better way. Don't let them trap you, if it's intentional.

13. TRUE   Try it and see.

14. FALSE Unfortunately, these decisions are sometimes overly influenced by financial considerations. Ethics, however, should be the prime mover.

15. FALSE Don't try it—it may cost you your job and your company a lot of trouble and money.

16. TRUE   Model the best, most ethical behavior you're capable of.

FIVE RULES FOR ETHICAL BEHAVIOR

As you read this book, you were presented with a variety of situations and issues in which ethics play an important part. (There are many more.) Hopefully, the result will be an increased awareness of the ethical ''mine field'' you face daily, and an increased understanding of how to navigate your way through it. Focusing on the following rules will be a good start.

1. Consider the needs of others, not just your own. Remember that you have to give to get, and that life is better when you live it as a win/win process.

2. Never forget just who you and your organization are. You are part of the community and a thread in the fabric of society. Don't do those things that common sense will tell you will cause it to unravel.

3. Obey rules, laws, and cultural standards, or get them changed. Remember, however, that you can be unethical without breaking the law. Use common sense and assess the potential damage of an unethical act or the violation of moral standards in advance. Violations are not worth it in the long run.

4. Test your thinking frequently. Ask yourself, ''Is this the right thing to do? Is it fair? Is it honest? Is there a better way?''

5. Don't lose your objectivity. This is a simple statement, but a tough order. What is right, what is fair, and what is in your best interest may be different things. Be sure you put your biases aside and look at all aspects of the issue.

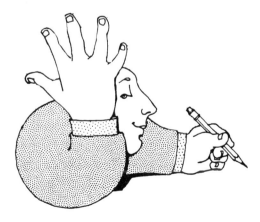

DESIGN A LIFE PLAN FOR THE FUTURE

> WHEN SCHEMES ARE LAID IN ADVANCE, IT'S SURPRISING HOW OFTEN CIRCUMSTANCES FIT IN WITH THEM.
>
> *Sir William Osler*

Include good ethical practices in your life plan—don't leave them to chance. Think through who you are and how you want to be known. What is the primary direction you want your life to take? Bringing these considerations to the surface, and keeping them there, will enable you to maintain your focus.

Ask yourself the questions listed below, jotting down your initial thoughts as you read them. Then wait two or three days before you read them again. Review them every week or two (mark the dates on your calendar) until you are comfortable with your answers, and you can begin to form a plan.

When you run into a problem of ethics, review this book along with these questions, your answers and your plan. As you learn new truths, add to your plan.

---

1. What are the really important things in my life?

_____

_____

_____

_____

2. What do I value most about my job?

_____

_____

_____

_____

DESIGN A LIFE PLAN FOR THE FUTURE (Continued)

3. What are the most important factors in my relationships with my boss? My peers? My employees?

_____

_____

_____

_____

4. What are some of the things that could happen on the job that would cause me to resign?

_____

_____

_____

_____

5. How would I like my boss to think of me?

_____

_____

_____

6. How would I like my employees to describe me to a person who has their total confidence?

_____

_____

_____

7. How much of my integrity would I trade for money? Promotion? Job security? The good will of management?

_____

_____

_____

DESIGN A LIFE PLAN FOR THE FUTURE (Continued)

8. Would I assign an employee to a job that I knew had not been made as safe as it should be?

_____

_____

_____

_____

9. Am I willing to lie to my employees to save face? To get a job done? To gain job security? To get a raise? To be promoted?

_____

_____

_____

10. Am I willing to deliberately work against associates to make them look bad and myself look good?

_____

_____

_____

11. Who do I want most to please?

_____

_____

_____

12. What kind of person do I consider unethical?

_____

_____

_____

DESIGN A LIFE PLAN FOR THE FUTURE (Continued)

13. What kind of people do I want to associate with on the job? Off the job?

_____
_____
_____
_____

14. Would I expect to be supported by my boss and co-workers if I played favorites with some of my employees?

_____
_____
_____
_____

15. Do I think it is all right to continually criticize and harass a peer or another work group?

_____
_____
_____
_____

16. How do I really feel about the equal employment opportunity laws? Can I and do I support them?

_____
_____
_____
_____

DESIGN A LIFE PLAN FOR THE
FUTURE (Continued)

17. Do I see discipline as a constructive process, designed to teach and to mold, or as justified punishment?

_____

_____

_____

_____

18. How would I describe an ethical person?

_____

_____

_____

_____

19. How do I want to be remembered by my associates?

_____

_____

_____

_____

20. How do I want to remember myself?

_____

_____

_____

_____

RESPONSES TO CASE STUDIES

RESPONSE TO CASE STUDY I—Harass Him Until He Quits
(page 10)

It's amazing how often this type of thing happens in organizations. The ethics involved seem perfectly clear, yet this ''solution'' is nothing more than a devious way for a manager to accomplish a personal goal. Harassment of this kind has nothing to do with performance, cost effectiveness, or the needs of the organization. In fact, it works against the best interests of the organization. It will be recognized for what it is by other employees, who will lose respect for management and the company. Also, a replacement will have to be recruited, hired and trained.

Why did the immediate supervisor so quickly accept this solution? Did he or she actually believe the action was warranted, or did fear of disapproval from above take control? Did the supervisor think it was all right simply because the decision was made at a higher level? Did he or she feel absolved of blame?

Whatever the reason, the immediate supervisor was placed in a ticklish position because to disagree with the boss might bring trouble. However, it is the strong opinion of the authors that this type of arbitrary action can often be prevented by simply offering some resistance on ethical grounds. A challenge, even a modest one, can be enough to bring the ethics into focus.

Supervisors who act responsibily when employees are in jeopardy, whether they like them or not, often bring reason to decisions, and prevent precipitous acts. In the long run, they are usually respected and appreciated. Supervisors who avoid the issue have little value to anyone when the chips are down.

RESPONSES (Continued)

RESPONSE TO CASE STUDY II—A Dilemma At The *Build Big* Company
(page 19)

J.B.'s request hit Sam hard, but he was prepared for the situation. He had been with J.B. almost from the beginning and was considered the balanced, conservative counterpart to J.B.'s creative and sometimes flamboyant entrepreneurial style. Sam knew exactly what was going on in some of the fee transactions and he also knew how high the stakes were for *Build Big*.

Sam had been in the building business for 20 years and his ethical standards had been tested more than once. He'd done a lot of thinking about what was most important to him through the years, and what he might do if a situation such as this one arose.

"J.B., I know you're carrying a big load," Sam might say, "but to be honest with you, I think doing this would add to the problem. Things like this tend to get you in deeper all the time. We might make it either way and we might lose it either way, but I have to tell you, I can't go down the wrong path on this one. I'll do anything that I can live with, but being honest has always been a big deal with me. It would hurt me a lot, but if *Build Big* starts bribing people, I can't work for you anymore."

RESPONSE TO CASE STUDY III—The Dance Of The Lemons
(page 26)

Gregory Samuels learned from his first important meeting with Linda Jensen that she was not an open communicator. He knew, therefore, he would have trouble doing his job to the best of his ability. He could not help wondering if poor communication was characteristic of senior management as a whole, and if poor downward communication had led to the reassignment of his predecessor. His worst fears were soon confirmed: communication from the top was sporadic, undependable, and incomplete. It was almost as if failure was the desired goal.

Gregory also made the effort to identify managers assigned to the ''Dance of the Lemons.'' He could not help noticing the lack of opportunity for them to make any significant contribution and their resulting loss of self-esteem. None of them could explain what had happened. If performance was the problem, it was never mentioned to them, and no suggestions were ever made for their improvement.

Gregory's final conclusion was that those engaging in the ''Dance of the Lemons'' were victims of an unethical management team who did not communicate their expectations or face up to performance issues with their subordinates. He decided to resign before he too became a victim of the system and ruined his own promising career.

Trust is essential to a productive work environment. It requires open, honest communication that increases awareness and builds cooperation. An environment of trust promotes loyalty and commitment to achieve the goals of the organization.

RESPONSES (Continued)

RESPONSE TO CASE STUDY IV—Just a Modest Change In The Records
(page 37)

Jenny returned the changed assessments to her boss with a note pointing out the inherent dangers in changing such records, and the matter was dropped. A short time later Jenny was reassigned to a less responsible position. The Vice President of Employee Relations said he needed someone in her job who could give him stronger support at the senior executive level.

Jenny got the message and left the company. She was convinced the request to change the records had come from a level above her boss and he had made no effort to resist it.

As a dedicated professional, Jenny did not wish to be associated with an organization with such limited values. She vowed never again to work with managers who had no compunction about destroying the career and economic well-being of others by falsifying information.

Jenny went on to have a very successful career and reflecting on her decision to leave her job, even though it meant hardship at the time, Jenny said, ''I have absolutely no regrets.''

RESPONSE TO CASE STUDY V—The Dueling Managers
(page 48)

Harry Hart knew the differences between Peter and Jan had exceeded all reasonable bounds. They had gone well beyond arguing differences of opinion and were now taking deliberate steps to destroy one another. They were doing heavy damage to the organization and were well on their way to destroying both their careers. He wondered if they hadn't dug themselves a hole they didn't know how to get out of.

Harry asked Peter and Jan to come to his office for a private meeting. He told them how much he thought of their abilities, and how much he appreciated and needed their contributions. ''But,'' he said, ''when you act the way you are acting now, and have been acting for some time, you don't help me or anyone else. Not only are you no good to me, you are destroying your respective organizations as well. How do you justify that?''

Peter and Jan both respected Harry and they knew he was a square shooter. His opinion mattered a great deal to both of them. They also knew he was right, and their defense was feeble.

Finally, Harry said, ''I don't want to lose either of you, but you're no good to me when you act the way you have been. Do you want to stay?''

Both Peter and Jan affirmed their desire to stay. ''O.K.,'' said Harry, ''on this condition. During the next two weeks I want you to sit down together and resolve your differences. Then come back to me and tell me your plan of action for working together in the future, and for restoring your organizations to the top performance they are capable of. And understand, I am not looking for lip service, I'm looking for the kind of managers I think you both can be. Will you do it?''

They agreed, and were back in two weeks with a workable plan they both could live with. They are making excellent progress toward full cooperation, and they are on the way to becoming the answer to a General Manager's prayer.

RESPONSES (Continued)

RESPONSE TO CASE STUDY VI—Is Process Insurance Enough?
(page 54)

The safety manager was quick to respond to the issue in this case. He said, ''Profitability is not the only issue here. We may be reimbursed for property loss, but what about the people who would be killed in a major accident? Are we going to tell their families not to worry, that they should be content with the proceeds from their insurance? What about the reactions from residents of the surrounding community whose lives or property might also be endangered? Do we want our presence here to be seen as an asset or a liability? What about our customers who are dependent upon us for their raw material?

The discussion then turned to the ethical implications of the issue, and the original safety package was adopted with all of its features. The venture was still highly profitable.

NOTES

NOW AVAILABLE FROM
CRISP PUBLICATIONS

Books • Videos • CD Roms • Computer-Based Training Products

If you enjoyed this book, we have great news for you. There are over 200 books available in the *50-Minute*™ Series. To request a free full-line catalog, contact your local distributor or Crisp Publications, Inc., 1200 Hamilton Court, Menlo Park, CA 94025. Our toll-free number is 800-442-7477.

Subject Areas Include:

Management

Human Resources

Communication Skills

Personal Development

Marketing/Sales

Organizational Development

Customer Service/Quality

Computer Skills

Small Business and Entrepreneurship

Adult Literacy and Learning

Life Planning and Retirement

CRISP WORLDWIDE DISTRIBUTION

English language books are distributed worldwide. Major international distributors include:

ASIA/PACIFIC

Australia/New Zealand: In Learning, PO Box 1051, Springwood QLD, Brisbane, Australia 4127   Tel: 61-7-3-841-2286, Facsimile: 61-7-3-841-1580
ATTN: Messrs. Gordon

Singapore: 85, Genting Lane, Guan Hua Warehouse Bldng #05-01, Singapore 349569   Tel: 65-749-3389, Facsimile: 65-749-1129
ATTN: Evelyn Lee

Japan: Phoenix Associates Co., LTD., Mizuho Bldng. 3-F, 2-12-2, Kami Osaki, Shinagawa-Ku, Tokyo 141   Tel: 81-33-443-7231, Facsimile: 81-33-443-7640
ATTN: Mr. Peter Owans

CANADA

Reid Publishing, Ltd., Box 69559-109 Thomas Street, Oakville, Ontario Canada L6J 7R4.   Tel: (905) 842-4428, Facsimile: (905) 842-9327
ATTN: Mr. Stanley Reid

Trade Book Stores: *Raincoast Books*, 8680 Cambie Street, Vancouver, B.C., V6P 6M9   Tel: (604) 323-7100, Facsimile: (604) 323-2600
ATTN: Order Desk

EUROPEAN UNION

England: *Flex Training,* Ltd. 9-15 Hitchin Street, Baldock, Hertfordshire, SG7 6A, England   Tel: 44-1-46-289-6000, Facsimile: 44-1-46-289-2417
ATTN: Mr. David Willetts

INDIA

Multi-Media HRD, Pvt., Ltd., National House, Tulloch Road, Appolo Bunder, Bombay, India 400-039   Tel: 91-22-204-2281, Facsimile: 91-22-283-6478
ATTN: Messrs. Aggarwal

SOUTH AMERICA

Mexico: *Grupo Editorial Iberoamerica*, Nebraska 199, Col. Napoles, 03810 Mexico, D.F.   Tel: 525-523-0994, Facsimile: 525-543-1173
ATTN: Señor Nicholas Grepe

SOUTH AFRICA

Alternative Books, Unit A3 Micro Industrial Park, Hammer Avenue, Stridom Park Randburg, 2194 South Africa   Tel: 27-11-792-7730, Facsimile: 27-11-792-7787
ATTN: Mr. Vernon de Haas